VIRGA

Togara Muzanenhamo was born to
Zimbabwean parents in Lusaka, Zambia,
in 1975. He was brought up in Zimbabwe,
and then went on to study in The Hague
and Paris. His work has appeared in
magazines in Europe, South Africa, the
United States and Zimbabwe, and was
included in Carcanet's anthology *New
Poetries* in 2002. He lives with his partner
and children in Harare.

Also by Togara Muzanenhamo from Carcanet

Gumiguru (2014)
Spirit Brides (2006)

VIRGA

Togara Muzanenhamo

CARCANET POETRY

First published in Great Britain in 2021 by
Carcanet
Alliance House, 30 Cross Street
Manchester, M2 7AQ
www.carcanet.co.uk

A CIP catalogue record for this book is
available from the British Library.

ISBN 978 1 80017 143 5

Typesetting by User Design, Illustration and Typesetting
Printed in Great Britain by SRP Ltd, Exeter, Devon

The publisher acknowledges financial
assistance from Arts Council England.

CONTENTS

Ndinopa basa rino nerudo kuna Rumbi naSanaa

Ola i ke ahe lau makani

'We are the fruits of the wind and have been seeded,
irrigated and cultivated by its craft'
– Lyall Watson

'As a result of the continuously inauspicious seas, which on the morning of Sunday, the 7th of this month, were once again particularly rough, the tip of the Mole and the lantern post also collapsed during that night. Considering how other facilities, for example those in Cape Town, are ravaged by the ocean, it can not come as a surprise that this harbour experiences similar rigours. The battle against the sea will be a continuous one.'

– Deutsch-Südwestafrikanische Zeitung, 12 June 1903

Tall and green-eyed. Garyupleh journeys out from Monrovia on
    word from Berlin.
The pulse of the steamer's engine pounding up into his palms
    through brass taffrails.
A black squall trailing off the smokestack – thinning out and staining
    the pale Atlantic sky.
The Harmattan whispers dryly off his skin. The Eduard Bohlen skirts
    the coast for Nifu
where crates of gin and barrels of beer are traded for more Kru. For
    men who know the sea.
Men chosen by his own hand. Figures sculpted from muscle. Solid
    youths with rounded
jowls he forcefully aligned to his squared chin when he stared deep
    into their eyes before
bolting his conscripts below deck. The ship's cargo hold ripe with an
    unguent perfume.
Away from the reef – the is sea flat. Silver glides of flying fish
    mirrored off its surface.
From the steamer's deck – he recalls his wife's somber wave amid a
    carnival of white
handkerchiefs. The young bride dropping her head then dropping
    her hand to her pregnant belly.
The image cuts deep. The thin white coast long lost beneath
    the horizon's blue shield.

The sun falls and sinks again. Vanishing beneath stars
    undulating in slow psalms
glistening off salt water – the German liner leagues from
    the beacon on Cape Palmas.
He avoids other passengers. Avoids the restaurant. The bar.
    Keeps to his berth.
Eats alone. Sleeps alone. Dreams of the steamship ploughing
    the South Atlantic Gyre –
spoon bow parting water – night waves falling back – blue with
    luminescent plankton –
the warm arm of the Guinea Current feeding life into
    Benguela's hibernal course.
Mossamedes comes. A fortress on brown cliffs. Then Port
    Negro with its long iron jetty.
Then Port Alexander – erased of thousands of flamingos –
    the sky grey above a grey sea.
More days pass. Colossal waves rise like dark liquid dunes or
    banks of rolling mercury.
The ship powers through them. Steel heaving and creaking.
    The deck awash with salt
till the waters calm and a ghostlike fog hugs the Skeleton
    Coast. Crossing Capricorn's
invisible belt – he wakes troubled from a dream: his wife
    cradling their lifeless newborn.
When the ship eventually reaches Swakopmund – he already
    longs for home.

The first night is cold. Miserable. The wind's bitter breath
    screams through gaps
in the makeshift cabin walls – the language of the southern
    sea constantly busy in his ear.
Unable to sleep he pulls on his boots. Walks out along the
    breakwater where whitecaps

rush up against rocks and spray down in fine breaths of rain. He sees
    the lantern post
stationed at the tip of the mole. And there by the simple beacon he
    stops. Arrested by
the sight of a dark heavy mass coming towards him – a shape he can
    not make out –
        a godless shape slowly approaching then morphing into a gang
        of men.

The lantern's light etches and enlarges the figures on a thick screen
    of mist.
Each silhouette becoming flesh. Each figure gaunt and naked as the
hour itself.

Eight shackled men. Two armed Schutztruppe at the rear.
    The stink of iron on wounds green with the ache of salt.
        The last of the men – a shackled ghost.
            Eyes burning red with revolt.

                                    *

    For hours he watches the lighthouse dialing out over the harbour –
the beacon's radial arm reaching deep into co-ordinates
        lost somewhere where the wind's conversation
            begins and ends with the sea.

    The sky aches. Marbled folds echoing white.
    His breaths draw back – dark with thunder.
And he knows a storm will come. And after the storm – more ships.
            Three thousand warmbloods.
            Fifteen thousand mausers.
            Fourteen thousand fresh men.

*

Why must you leave.
Why must you constantly go.
Why is the sail
masted to your soul.
A warm breeze rolls over Nyanpue's naked shoulders –
dark clouds rolling thick over Montserrado. And Garyupleh fears the day
their firstborn will come – the child coming in his absence.
Then what would be done
if others charged in from other villages or lands –
flared nostrils – eyes burning in the shade of cotton trees –
riders galloping and spitting fire and cutting men down over beach sand –
dismounting and seizing girls and women and
holding boys back to
witness blood fall anew –
just as he'd been sewn among his own.
And holding his wife
he says nothing and stares into the thatched dark
and thinks of all the journeys he's taken
that brought him back to his own shores.
Journeys that have come with every curse
and blessing of sun and rain.
Journeys of men and states and rites of passage.
And when he feels Nyanpue's breath
fold into its own course of gentle sleep –
he closes his eyes and sees
the sky washing off the decks
of ships he knows
will never sail clean.

*

Born to the sea.
Raised by the sea.
He sits listening to the rhythmic hymn
of salt and surf on rock and sand.

Storm petrels painted faint on the horizon.
Rain falling
into the harbour's ear.

*

He can not cleanse his mind
of the men staggering shackled
over the knurled wash of the mole.

Walking back to the wooden barracks
the mist thickens to a heavy fog –
and the lantern glows somewhere

with a dull amniotic light –
the sea's cold murmuring chorus
lost between midnight and the dawn.

The vague sound of a wind motor
pumps. His feet lift caked with sand
swept over sidewalks beside new firms:

Damara & Namaqua Trading Co.
Wecke & Voigts. Erhardt & Schultz.
A closed restaurant. Dim-lit private

apartments. He too is cloaked in the brume
of what is here. He feels his heart
sink to his gut like a boulder tumbling

through an endlessly charged depth.
And as he walks – cold moisture
collects on his lips. The sea's

and sky's condensation salted
with a terrible promise he can not
pronounce. The agony of unsaid

prayers rushing up and crashing
against rock – taking to the sky
and falling back. Becoming mist.

MISTRAL

'I'll win the Tour de France provided I'm not murdered before we get to Paris.'

Maurice Garin, 1904

«Nous fussions morts pour Dreyfus. Dreyfus n'est point mort pour Dreyfus.»

Charles Péguy, Notre Jeunesse

By evening the rush
of the wind washing over leaves had calmed.
The week before – Lyon had seen us in with hoodlums –
four masked men in a car – brass knuckles polished with spit.
When midnight came it came with ceremony and flags –
        beer and wine flowed
to get us off – off on our way down the road
    that brightened with the scent of pollen and summer dust –
        the sun bouncing angrily off its surface
    as it took us towards the pass
where crowds waited seeding the route with iron tacks and broken glass.
    This. Their country. Col de Grand Bois.
Saint-Étienne. Annonay. Lyon. This. Their mountain pass.
Col de La République waging war on us.
Our bodies wrenched to our machines – gears and chains turning heavily –
    elbows tucked back to defend our ribs
through the violent tunnel roaring ripe with rage.
    Then. Five shots rang out.
        And the mob fled.
    Leaving Fauré to vanish up the road –
up and over the pass – into his town. Heart pumping for all he was worth.
            Breath owed to the land's history.
    Just as those who forged heavy templates
        and set the age old press
            to print the story
        of another race.

ÖXARÁ

for GerðurKristny

i Þingvellir
   after Þórarinn B. Þorláksson

Rubbing his thumb over his forefinger
   he lifts both digits to his nostrils
and closes his eyes and retraces the zephyr trailing off his forearm
with the scent of the wild mare. And begins to sketch.
   The horse glancing downstream.
      The river pewter blue.
         Farmhouse and church
            reflected off the river's surface
               with the evening sky.

ii Prestsdæturnar
    after Ásgrímur Jónsson

Without questioning the river's source
he studies the gentle flow surging freely –
   shadows and light
      curving below his raised arm.

   Charcoal to paper. Shirtsleeves rolled up.
Cumulus membranes shielding the landscape from the sun.
   From the hilltop he follows the current's slow meander
      to two women in conversation

on the river bank. One bathing her feet. The other leaning back.
　　Both figures as casual as the pale smoke rising
　　　　from the vicarage chimney –
　　the grey air gaining height
　　　　　and thinning out like prayer.

iii　　　Drekkingarhylur

　　　Sunlight penetrates the gin clear pool.
　　Silhouettes emerge. Transient shadows
warp through currents in shapeless forms.
　　　　She studies the flow.
For hours. Days. Weeks. Returns after months
　　　　　　and lifts her phone with new eyes
and films the haunted light churning deep
　　　with twisted contours
　　　　　constantly reaching up
　　　　　and continuously
　　　　　　being dragged down again.

iv　　　*Thórir*

Who rides the wind at night.
　　Charts the landscape's breath.
　　　Warm or cold over history's arm.
Shadow tattooed on air –
　　translated through blood.
　　　Forest and moorland.
　　　　Rain – stone and earth
　　　　　running along banks
　　　　　　wet with the river's name.

'The voyage began. My mother and I shared the nursing; he would not allow anyone else near him and we gladly, though with heavy hearts, took entire charge. What he suffered from most was the alternation of a sub-normal with a high temperature, which he reduced by violent perspiration.'

Alma Mahler

'Wohin ich geh? Ich geh, ich wand're in die Berge
Ich suche Ruhe für mein einsam Herz.'

Der Abschied, Das Lied von der Erde

Like a mournful bassoon – the SS *Amerika*'s horn blasts once –
the liner leaving New York en route for Cherbourg –
  the composer half lucid in his suite –
    lower jaw loose – temples wet with fever –
  the world already at work on his obituary.
Across the Atlantic – Europe bursts wild with spring.
Swathes of light flood his mind with a rugged beauty
  his weakened heart guards with fervour –
the cold shadowed waves fading thin
with the open glare of the ocean's classical tones.
  Again he slips into a fevered stare where he sits in his hut
listening to pine forests humming in the valley below:
  the sun departing behind the mountains –
    the evening descending with its shadows:
  slow strings over soft strokes of the tam-tam –
    woodwinds and the spare pluck of a mandolin.
He knows death is not easy. Knows the brief shadows of the young.
  His own breath floating sharp over the edge of the world.
    And it all comes back to him: the last Toblach summer –
the walks through fields wild with gentians and chanterelle and cep –
    stretches of sunlight twisting wild off the lake –

the smell of ink – the air wet with a stranger's musk –
another's breath resonating somewhere off Alma's skin…
the sea gently settles with violins and French horns
and a catch of stars glitters on the waves
in a way stars always do and will forever.
Forever.
Forever.

SUN DOGS

The Japanese polar exploring ship Kainan Maru arrived at Wellington yesterday.
Members of the expedition state that they did not go to look for the South Pole, but
confined themselves to scientific exploration.

Professor Takeda, when asked if Captain Scott had reached the Pole, answered
that Captain Scott was well equipped, and might have attained his object.

Sydney Morning Herald, 25 March 1912

We found ourselves heading north on a flat frozen plain
not made for the human voice.
    Seven men and a team of Karafuto-ken –
        hauling sleds back to the Bay of Whales.

    The wind came in hard. Forcing us to turn. Lean.
Shoulder its force. And still we pushed on into the white dissonant howl
        that also pushed back – threatening to pull
each man deep into the hold of the magnetic south.

Before this – only a few dared to imagine any pledge to the pole.
    And when we walked at our limit on the limits of the world
        we knew to turn back and return to the ridge
where conquest had burnt bright in our hearts.

After three banzai we left the Hinomaru flapping violently
    on a new Yamato Yukihara. As we walked – we leaned
into the noise that doubled our weight and dragged at our heels.
    The cold coiling our blood into blue maps of steel.
Each step forward erasing each step left behind.

*

When the wind drew back its merciless arm – a white calm
fell flat and the ice field sat still like a blank page
and the sound of our names rang clear for the first time in days.

For a long while we surveyed the scope of the desert –
the rim of the jagged horizon pressed hard against the bright sky.
Then we walked on. Our pace now easier on the breath.

Both the map-work of the heart and needle of the compass
navigating a silence thrown out open before us – a silence
so quiet that when we slept we woke from wordless dreams.

*

    A warm evening years
after the Tokyo parade and the Emperor's death.

    My wife asleep in my arms.
A breeze at play on shoji screens as I drift off and dream

    of ghosts and the white continent.
Dogs burrowed deep beside the tent – all asleep –

    the tent's canvas flap parted to reveal
the midnight sun squatting low on the ridge –

the sun burnished bright like a yellow amethyst.

From the lip of the ridge the sun never leaves
    but hovers above the serrated edge
waiting for straps to lash sledges –
    for dogs to bark and strain tow lines and move –

only then does the sun slightly rise
    as the campsite vanishes

back into an undivided landscape bright
    with atonal calm –

our shadows scribbled over our shoulders
    like illegible scripts of wire.

Along a stretch fractured black with veined crevasses –
    the weight of the continent groans

like a beast waking from a century's sleep.
    We turn back and listen and say nothing –

        continuing north over the ice field

till the sun angles down and a hand falls on my shoulder.
    Without a word we remove our goggles and look out

where the sun hangs delicate and strange – a bright mass
    with two parhelia burning at her flanks –

the vision drawing us to stare out to where
    men had only dreamed to roam –

two bright halos linking a trinity
    that had come as quietly as it would go –

the air dismantling the miracle – and soon enough
    a breeze stirred and the horizon darkened

    with stratospheric clouds

and frozen dust lifted off our heels as we walked again.

The noon sun seemingly holding still
    beneath a pearl nacreous veil.

Queen's Gambit

> '*One usually makes blunders for good reasons, for instance because of over exertion,*
> *divided attention, or some other hidden failing in one's mental makeup. On this*
> *occasion the Cuban sun was to blame. It had intoxicated me.*'
>
> Emanuel Lasker, 4 April 1921, Havana

Forty two years had passed since chess matches and card games
    for small stakes at Café Kaiserhof. He'd left Neumark
for Berlin. Gained prominence in St Pertersburg. Montreal. Paris. London.
    Emigrated to New York and was now leaving Amsterdam

    with Martha aboard the *Hollandia*. The journey – three weeks
from the feldgrau waters of the Dutch port. The North Sea's epeiric hold
opening out to the vast Atlantic where shapes of sky and water loosened
    to join trade routes washed bright with cyanic light.

Plough winds swept over the Strait of Florida – but the Gulf of Mexico
    stirred mildly and gave nothing more. The *Hollandia* finally
entering a bay once known for the sound of fortress bells and canon fire.
The Caribbean Sea cresting the esplanade and sea wall of the Malecón.

The grand master had arrived. And though the City of Columns
welcomed him – it's citizens still reserved every prayer
    for the Spanish officer's son. The match was on.
    Each man to face the other as both challenger and champion.

*

When they met the air was humid. The Union Club packed.
    No-one said a word. Only the audience's breath caught the ear.
Sugar barons in white linen suits perfumed front row seats
    with clouds of blue expensive Corojo smoke.

Every eye trained on the clock beside the board on the wall.
    The clock waiting to give and divide time and turn thought
into movements and ideas and images that would run wild over
    calm memorised scenes multiplied like grains of rice.

For years the world had waited on these two men to meet.
And when the German eventually lifted his hand –
    the audience drew their breath as they watched him hesitate.
        Intoxicated by the Cuban sun.

Chaturanga

Dust currents.
    Salt.
   Porcelain and gunpowder. Mountain paths
     drawing language over routes
of ivory and silk –
    a canvas
      where sketches of empires
  took form beneath
    biradi trees –
      sketches migrating
        to territories
  where elephants become bishops
and armies expand with knights financed by pious kings
      through latitudes and centuries
        forging everything down
          to the modern game
  where the board is still a field where wars rage
      to own territories
       and routes –
        where enclaves and dominions lay
      controlled by lords
    whose hearts are
  ruled by queens
    shifting beneath veils
      of smoke.

King's Indian Attack

'How Do You Make a Computer Blink?'
New York Times, Friday 2 May 1997

He has this recurring dream of the Turk –
    the cold-eyed genius flown into New York
        reciting algebraic verse with a digital tongue.

He sleeps in the Plaza troubled by its electronic
    shifting eye. The rapid binary pulse of its work.
When he wakes he knows only fools ignore dreams of their foes.

*'I am torn between the desire to tell you one of the most thrilling experiences of my life
and keeping my agreement with Mr. Arthur Hind. I have been thinking about it ever
since I saw in the magazines that his famous Guiana stamp was up for auction again.
I am an old man, Mr. Dietz, and I lead a quiet retired life with only an occasional
automobile trip partly across the country, my days of excitement are long over, yet the
excitement that telling my story is giving me makes me think I have no reason to feel
guilty about my agreement, since Mr. Hind has passed away and no one will ever
know who I am. Perhaps I am indulging in a weakness, the weakness of human nature
in wanting somebody to know that 'I had one too'. Yes Mr. Dietz, I had one too!'*
Anonymous letter to *Stamp and Cover Collector's Review*, October 1938

'Damus Petimus Que Vicissim'

From Allegany to Oneida – a grey curtain of rain blurred the county roads.
    The Highboy rumbling east into Utica where I set up
        at the hotel and telephoned Hind. All day
    no answer. The next day the same. But when evening came

I heard the cold click of the receiver and the grunt of his name.
    Then the sound of listening… When he spoke again –
        he gave directions to a house on
    the corner of York and Main where a double-leafed door opened

as the sky burst open and doused the street behind my back.
    I stepped into the vestibule. Hung up my coat.
        Followed him up a flight of stairs
    into a wainscoted room – panels fitted tongue and groove.

From hip-height to the ceiling – the glint of book spines. Perfumes of oak
   and shellac and burnt honey and tobacco smoke.
      I opened my satchel. Pulled the album
   out of its oilskin pouch. Parted the leafs beneath the desk lamp

and watched him adjust the lampshade as he bowed to study the barque –
   the square rigged silhouette sailing stark
      against a pale magenta sky – the clerk's
   initialed signature scribbled dirtily into the darkened sails.

Hind stepped back. Slowly drew his eye up from the imperforated print
   and studied me studying him. It was then that I became
      aware that only one could exist.
   So when the sum for the right of ownership floated off his lips –

I nodded. He picked up the stamp. Struck a match. And a phosphorous
   kiss sent the ship on its way – out along waves
      mirrored on horizons wild like Ravel's
   seascapes – flames weaving darkness into the ship's squared sails.

And before anything could be said – all was ashes – the barque
   reduced to a secret settling quiet at our feet –
      the last faint notes of flames lost
   in gentle breaths of smoke shivering out into slow calm waves…

When I left Utica – the early morning light crept up over the hotel
   and fell bare on cold tram rails. The streets empty.
      Shop windows blank. And I drove.
   Drove southwest. Darts of cold drizzle striking the windshield –

the Highboy buckling through the black mucklands of Canastota –
out to Syracuse via Madison – Genesee – Pennsylvania –
and further south through towns where
mill wheels slowed over cooling kilns giving little or nothing back.

There were never reasons to make this memory.
  The moon slipping quietly behind clouds.
    All sense of land gone.
      E nós poderíamos ser assim para sempre...
    Ocean salt. Wooden oars pulling back.
      Each stroke stirring something of the journey.
        E nós deviamos ter este lugar na mente...
      A sense of rain builds in the distance.
    White ions charged then suddenly sprayed
        across an endless sky.
  E manteremos esse lugar em nossos corações para sempre...

BHARATHANATYAM

'There is no need to say that before she entered the field, the art was dead and gone or that it saw a renaissance only when she started to dance or that she created anything new that was not there before'.

— E. Krishna Iyer

You don't have to dance, for if you just walk accross the stage, it will be enough. People will come to watch you just do that.

— Anna Pavlova

The Bishop of Madras said
he'd attended a benediction –

a spiritual flame burning

off his collar –

dust

lifting from bare heels –

every movement

entwined

within
the arms
of a banyan tree.

BENEATH THE SWALLOW'S NEST

for Jackie Cahi and Robin Wild

Viel gold'ne Bilder sah ich um mich schweben;
das schöne Traumbild wird zur Totenklage. –
Mut! Mut! – Was ich so treu im Herzen trage,
das muß ja doch dort ewig mit mir leben!
        – Theodor Körner, 'Abschied vom Leben'

Perhaps these young men have nothing more to lose…
what is to become of a generation to which Society
offers no social existence and which has only one thing
left to look to, a single day's glory, the swiftly tarnishing
highlight of a single hour? To be a bit of a hero, a bit
of a soldier, sportsman or record breaker, a gladiator,
victorious one day, defeated the next…
        – *Grindelwald Echo*, July 24, 1936

Only this wind. The darkness and this mountain.
Our limbs twisted. Faded back against the black
rock face. Air sharpened cold with a razored rain
slashing over the Eiger's spine – the same frac
tured air that washed us off the ledge. If I live
to see the dawn – I know it will not be by prayer
but by something else spawned from promises
the Wengen Boys made before they left: *Survive*
the night! Their calls faint off the Alpine air.
So I hold on to survive – twisting in the darkness.
The blind starless sky staring upon the mountain.

*

In youth we felt the föhn fall from the seared sky
and the air became our medium. Paths and crags
returned the world to a natural pace with musky
perfumes of grass. From then we knew not to ask
why turning streams mourned over bells tolling
in the shade beneath mountain ash – why lakes
grew large as seas mirroring skies blown wide
by war. Here I'd find joy – slung to ropes rolling
back in hymns off each step up mountain peaks
white as arsenic – sentinels guarding the old divide
of gods and men. The Aryan sun warm as whisky.

*

The air roars off rocks with a violent berceuse.
Memories screaming tirelessly through dreams.
This is all everything is – air screaming through
thoughts of men who scaled Bavarian peaks to kiss
the feet of gods – where winds whispered true
in tribute of mortal men who grappled the stars'
terrain. Memories of the sun's golden bugle
playing slow in muscular tones through valleys
where each laboured step drew us up into the air's
fragile cage. Faces browned with a burnt veil.
Lips split. Bloody and raw. Sparks in our eyes
locked to the earth. Hearts burning with peace.

*

And that search for freedom threatens my being.
The night's edge sharp. Cutting through time.
Wired emotions running through me – turning
into rushes of hope starved of religion and rhyme.
How it's all changed from climbing naked routes
to soothe the burning call for solitude – the elixir
of triumph sweet on our tongues – the mountain
air thin and blue. Bights of hemp. Studded boots.
Unveiled heights with views breathtakingly clear.
Each summit's point felling us to our knees again.
An unmeasured sense of worth saturating our being.

*

Mercy. The weight of death draws on me hard.
Hope falls away. Each dream painted black
by strokes belted out from the evening blizzard.
A callous wind lashing against the ancient rock.
Its air at my temples drawing out every memory
I own – and every crucial moment I have lived
turning back to mock what I'd failed to foresee –
the very will of my soul drained like a tributary
ebbing out into something few have survived.
The wind's cold strokes strike with misery.
Mercy. The weight of death draws on me hard.

*

I still remember the warmth of my mother's lips
pulling away from my cheek – the Bavarian air
crisp with the summer sun falling wet off wisps
of matted hair – and all I thought of was the Eiger –
the sheer wall standing high – wind whistling
over ice – songs composed without words –
music over earth set in beautiful staves of grief
impended by war. And now this same whistling
stirs my heart with this thought that explodes
with a dark reversal of breath – a gasp of life
above the dead weight twisting beneath my hips.

*

Three men are dead. Men linked to me by fate.
Up sour paths our dreams were sweet. Years
of toil up ivory peaks. The lyric march of feet
counting down the days to the eventual hour
of our assent. Two ropes were manned and firm
-ly gripped till Willy looked up and took a blow
from loose falling rock. Two days we struggled.
On the third we were forced to descend to the arm
of the ledge – our progress tiresome and slow.
When we reached the traverse without a lead
to take us back – we stood troubled by our fate

staring out on to the rock listening to the slate
grey air lashing back with nothing to give –
the air then beginning to turn to a loud white
embittered scream tasked with trying to deceive
our course – the weather's assault constantly
at ends to break our will. And there – where
we stood was where it all mattered – staring out
across the pegged ropeless face that mockingly
stared back – reminding us how we left – where
we unthreaded the traverse – hemp slipping out
of the final piton's eye – and sealing our fate.

*

It was a virtuoso piece of climbing. Andreas' heart beating hard and white off his breath. Every muscle tense and ready to flex for the first vital kick-start that launched him into the air like a wingless angel. Each brief flight screwing his face into a tight grimace as he swung down then came up carrying a purpose that held each of us still as he flowed and spliced the wind's cold orchestral lore – the ice-trebled sky sketched bone grey above the Rote Fluh. Again he pitched and soared with a purpose owed to the air – his flight fresh off the pulse of his heart –

the cold scrape of iron etched off each kick-start – catches of wet sparks flinted beneath the heavy sky. Again: pitch and swing launching him over the ice skirt – edging him over the traverse – a speck swinging high above wooden decks where scopes focused up from the hotel and herder's pass – distance's omission muting the hammer on the piton before he soared out again across the rock face – us simply watching him from the ledge – him flying and falling in succession. Each flight out-daring anything else in our pursuit. Each breath flushed white off each beat of his heart.

*

Without faith there is no deliverance. Without
hope all faith is blind. The earth refuses my
body. The heavens suspend my weight. Doubt
and fear shadow my soul. Time is my enemy.
How can man live between the sky and earth –
locked in the delicate balance of falling and flight.
And though we have scaled rock and hacked
the sky to launch ourselves to the sun – the earth
will not let go. Even the sky's temporal light
waits. Not wanting – but knowing the abstract
meaning of every light that eventually goes out.

*

And somehow the sky will glow when the dawn creeps crisp and slow across the mountain face. And true to their promise the Wengen boys return and call my name. And I will call back with a voice as fresh as theirs. Beneath the Swallow's Nest the brothers will rise and haul themselves up to where I twist in slow turns between the earth and sky – our eyes meeting with an unrehearsed chorus of joy as the sun reels up into a clean blue sky that quickly saturates with every colour of faith – waiting to burst loud with the anthem of the dawn.

THE TEXAN

James A. Mattern, noted flier, was granted permission by the Commerce Department today to make an aerial search for the Russian aviators believed lost in the Arctic wilderness.

In making the search, Mr. Mattern will be returning a favor from Sigismund Levanevsky, leader of the Russian flight.

The Russian went to Mr. Mattern's rescue a few years ago when the American aviator was marooned in Northern Siberia.'

Pittsburg Post-Gazette, 15 August 1937

From Weeks Field the sun hangs uncertain.
>The air sharpened by the curse of razored winds –
sheets of sky and sea layered silver with ice.
>Each hour vanishes into broken distances.
The shape of the world formed on each breath – oiled drops
>>shivering wet off rivets – the engine
>>>moaning dark at the wrists.

Evening swivels west as the Texan turns.
>Her wings banked shallow above the ocean's crust –
pedals and levers at their place for altitude.
>Through angled glass – the quiet world of a frozen
solitude – a vast naked bridge of bruised light bridging continents –
>>white skirts of blind speed beaming
>>>over lengths of desolate prose.

The radio crackles white with endless noise.
>The ceiling of the world dry with fate.
And banking into the failing light – he remembers the furled
>wisps sparked by whips of air turning up as the Russian landed –
then – the rattled chop of blades as the plane left for Nome –
>the compass marked for home and all
>>the vaporous qualities of life.

Time sinks fast. Darkening with ancient layers
        creaking below – unsaid prayers the dead
have set to verse. A grey breath of air slips heavily
        off each wing – the flat drone of the engine working
the mind to paint the final flight with a grieved art – the soul's white feathers
        burning bright as the prototype rolled and crashed
            deep into the heart of the unknown.

POIDS

'The step has gone away, the walker has fallen silent
on the dial of imitation
the pendulum throws its instinctive load of granite.'
            René Char (Le Marteau sans Maitre, Pierre Boulez)

'Ce n'était pas sans inquiétude tant pour le piano que pour nos oreilles, que
l'on s'était rendu à ce concert: on s'attendait même à voir la salle remplie
de sportifs enthousiastes. Micheline Ostermeyer n'est-elle pas championne de
lancement de poids?'

The air is alive with colour.
Emblems of nations. De Coubertin's rings embroidered
        fresh on silk rippling above lime-lined tracks.
    Cinders damp under athletes' feet –
        spikes kissed black with incendiary dirt.

When her name is called she stands and waves to the crowd
    and warms up by stretching her legs.
She interlinks the fingers of both hands.
    Rolls her wrists. Her chalked palms
swimming over smooth flesh like two carpal fish
        locked in a sacred ritual.

    She picks up the black weight.
Breathes deep and exhales and steps into the circle.
Her heart drumming hard.
    Pulse echoing loose off the breeze.

    With her eyes closed – she steadies herself.
The cool iron sphere buried beneath her jaw.
        Leaping forward.
            She throws her arm out to the world.

*

Each ionised note floats lightly off the wireless.
Liszt's air flowing through French neighborhoods in Tunis –
staves of bright Hungarian light sparked off nimble fingertips.

And what was said at times – behind closed doors of salons
and conservatoires – about her Grecian build and heavy touch –
is now forgotten and lost somewhere in the grandeur of the hall.

And when the music stops and pages turn through acoustic coughs
of gentlemen beside trophy wives and mistresses laced with the slow
heavy burn of real pearls fragranced by real perfumes –
she steadies herself. Loosens and rolls her wrists and feels the air

*

fall cool off her palm –
        the shot
pivoted somewhere
    off the sole's return.
            A note hanging briefly.
            Waiting.
                To hit the earth.

The City of Winds stirs a restless need in him.
His breath heavy with thoughts he swears to take to his grave.
He stands alone. Stares up at the window.
The window's cool electric light echoing off the sea's rhythmic breeze.
Walking through Martyrs' Lane
he'd heard the olive trees whispering beneath the naked sky –
stars twisting high above a city numb with adrenalin.
Each footstep quickens his pulse till he reaches her street.
He holds his head. Stumbles back and hides in the night-shadows –
the old stone walls pressed up sturdy on his shoulders –
a thick iron railing squared against the small of his back.
From the dark he watches the lace drapes roll out with the breeze –
the sound of the sea soft off the building's solid Persian masonry.
As mists of drink begin to clear in his head –
he rights his stance and begins to walk away.
But as he turns on his heel –
the window throws out the silhouette
of a man – the naked shadow staining the glass.
He stands still and can not look away.
Enraged – he feels the need to kneel.
So he kneels.
But can not kneel for long.
And soon finds himself scaling up a wall.
A wall he initially
did not know as a wall.
A wall that delivers
him into a small unlit garden.

CORRESPONDENTS

01°28'09"S 78°49'03"W

With a change of clothes
    in his rucksack
he rode the Suzuki towards the black cloud
crowning the mountain's peak –

the motorbike heading up
    the gravel road –
passing tour buses and tourists' cars –
passing women and children and men on foot

all walking up a path like strange
    pilgrims en route
to a geographic coordinate he'd first
seen tattooed across the naked hip of a woman

he'd heard about but hadn't seen
    until the two strangers met
in the lobby of some shot-up hotel in downtown Beirut.
A woman without a name until they

woke to a ringing phone: *Si. Maria!*
    She said then proceeded to speak in Arabic.
Three weeks they met in her room. Drank gin. Fucked.
The air outside riddled with the soundtrack

of distant gunfire.
    Mogadishu. Tripoli.
Baghdad. Kosovo. Over the years they found each other –
exhausted – typing the keys of war.

And this is what they were bred for.
    Cresting the frontlines.
Watching the world play out. Concrete
and dirt punched hard with the vengeance of modern artillery.

When her convoy was hit –
    three armoured trucks blown up –
fifteen killed on the spot – he knew nothing of her whereabouts for weeks.
The night before all this – they lay in bed

and spoke of the heart of the earth
    and before they fell asleep
she revealed the secret of the coordinates tattooed on her hip.

And now he rides to Carell Hut.
    Gravel beneath the wheels pitched cold.
        His promise hauling him up the elevated road.
    A change of clothes wrapping the urn
that will empty out in swift grey turns off of Chimborazo's peak.

VIRGA

'*Se dirá que tenemos*
en uno de los ojos mucha pena
y también en el otro, mucha pena
y en los dos, cuando miran, mucha pena…'
César Vallejo

Must have been the thunder
rolling down the mountainside that made the clown
lead the children to higher ground –
the circus tent left behind
with all its theatre – then swallowed whole three minutes later.
Fifty years on you can still see
four half buried palm trees.
Fragments of the cathedral wall beside the old cemetery.
A wrecked bus raised like a strange crustacean riding a wave of rock.
Hard to imagine how it all came down.
The black rush off Huascarán's shoulder. Mud. Ice. Boulders.
Everything sealed beneath the earth.
A statue of Christ with open arms stares down from the old cemetery's hill.
From the high ground – three hundred children
had watched the highland town erased with all they'd known.
The dead never exhumed.
Only names floating dark with grief.
The veiled altocumulus above our heads –
drifting
and thinning out
over Callejón de Huaylas.

HOBIKI BUNE

'...*the utopian possibility of a space for these two girls [in] love,*
even when there is no space other than in the depths of their own hearts.'
Yoshiya Nobuko, *Yellow Rose*

and she'd promised she would never let it happen again
    but allows her lover's chin
to slip into the atoll of her collarbone –
    her eyes locked on the fishermen sailing in
        with the morning sun –

    the air running crisp and clean
over Sagami Bay – the view pristine
    where they stood on the mountain –

    the sea sewn
    bright with salt

a cold palm snatches the heat off her skin
    as a warm vulnerable whisper asks forgiveness

    and nothing else

the fishermen sailing into the harbor – white sails falling loose
            and gently rolling down
beneath a cloud of gulls ascending with the rising sun

GOUGH

Standing on The Glen
he reels in the line
and stares out
beyond Dell Rocks
where silver skies
map a route to the Cape –
where the Atlantic washes up
over the continent's foot.
Staring out over the bay
he breathes the salt air
taking winter home –
where the west winds' current
will spray up from rocky shores
and slither into beds of fynbos
then rise white like prayer
above the peninsular
where iron skies
are knitted with the thread wire
of migratory birds
diving through Morse code
and radio channels
carrying forecasts and news
back to where he stands –
a world away
from the world –
radiosonde and balloon
miles above The Glen.

BLUEGRASS COUNTRY
for E. W.

'In about 70 years, you can place my body here'
  – Eddie Arcaro, the reinterment of Isaac Murphy, Faraway Farm,
Lexington, 1967

'One more mighty plunge, and with knee, limb and hand,
I lift my horse first by a nose past the stand.
We are under the string now – the great race is done
And Salvator, Salvator, Salvator won!'
  Ella Wheeler Wilcox, 'How Salvator Won'

I.   *Churchill Downs*
1891

The sky curves fast – burning over iron rails.
Dirt flicking up beneath the polished clap of sweat.
  Reins drawing each breath blunt from the sternum.
Knees in. The sun loud. Hats gripped in hands waving wild
  from the grandstand – applause composed of timeless stuff.
    Jockeys bow hard to the mane.
The short catch of leather off muscle.
          The sky bending out straight
            where speed is held.
          Man and horse flat out.
          The weight of flames shivering in the eyes
            of rider and beast.
              Breaths of fire
            spilling wet off the lips of a fevered crowd.

II. Cemetery of the Union Benevolent Society
1955

Tangled vines breathe over cool backs of stone.
Sun-veined nutsedge bound tight over dates eroded by time.
    The earth rests wired and neglected. Another summer comes to pass.
The dead lie without names – the link of age rusted with ankle chains
        running quiet into a fog of clouded musket fire.
    The railroad sings loud. Junkyard metal lies twisted by sunlight.
Beyond a torn trodden fence – Lexington sits forged by southern prayer –
      Baptist words rising from the heart –
           burdened songs sung
     for the leaden-paced march into each quick-silvered twilight
       reined by the whip's black hymn –
           songs sung by those
              who'd walked the dark
           roads only to learn
              to run –
                then ride alone.

III.   *The Hamilton Piece*
1980

From
Jordan's Row
the slow silver light
stands solid in its place –
a laboured
gleam
sloping off narrow shoulders
with an unassumed grace:
rider
standing sure
and strong.
Jacket and
crop
in hand.
Knee-high
boots.
Long
legs
planting
a
silver
stride
set firm
on the base of the American equine turf.

IV.   Charging Shadow
Circa 1964

Always this dream – the
immortal flick of wind –
the dark sediment caking
our mouths. Always this
feeling of time sitting flat
like crust turning soft in
our brains – the earth
wet with a dour embrace.
Wandering footfall tears
through the union of fo-
liage and sun – a breath of
earth and stone thicken-
ing with an inquisitive
charge. *How do the dead
defend themselves* – cross-
armed – hollow-breasted –
muscle undone by the
wet-rotting song of time.
For years we lay lost –
hugged tight by mounds
of ungoverned earth –
squat nameless blocks
knotted above our heads
till the shovel's eye sunk
its blade and tipped and
rose with pure betrayal.

V. The Ungiving

And for a while the darkness is new again –
    the earth heavy with the ungiving spring.
     Who will hear the gentle spats of rain
spit on earth and turn songs we'd forgotten to singing
       hymns rooted to trees sweet
       with the blood of pinioned fruit –
       fruit hung from boughs – swinging
     swollen and ripe – casually falling
beyond the view of this plain.

VI.   *Faraway Farm, Lexington*
1967
                        Lucy Murphy: 1868–1910

The mineral sound of bone rings heavy
with each natural layer of calcium – the wind
sweeping low with Kentucky's prayers.
Paddocks and fields roll out to naked views
where troubled mares slip off to foal
the sun over fresh snow – the moon setting
    again – drawing me to think of you.

        In simple terms light is inverted –
        the air folded to compact earth –
        the world another place – another life
        where veined roots are cut blind –
        the white thread of matrimonial love
        severed from the jasmine bone.

And so the seat is rich – yet the throne
            quiet on the template of legendary
worth – a wealth of praise bowing with
            the humility of stone. And where
time sits is far divorced from the heart –
            the air brittle with bone set beneath
dust and snow – the matter of flesh
            resolved by the earth – the matter of us
            turned again – incomplete by the vogue
                of time – my head in your arms forgotten –
            the chalkstone dirt stretch heavy with calcium –
                the track drumming hard with hoof and applause –
the grief of Kentucky's prayers – the black-foaled

stars giddy where our hearts lay
quiet in the brier-tangled shadows –
the music of unwanted distance grating loud
with what can only be
the memory of an intimate age.

VII.   *Call to the Post*
2011

Kentucky Horse Park

The memorial stands to crown Man o'War.
   Secretariat sired by distant blood.
      Royal stakes and garlands
      trickling dew to gather
   where each chestnut colt stands
proud – dawn folding back its copper hood.

Morning light is simple. Each warm stable
   heavy with the tang of manure –
      blue starlings whistling –
      the air fresh with subtle
   notes of perfumes and light falling
heavier and heavier on this portrait of nature

carved into art with the patient hands of a dream –
   a dream tended with a gardener's
      care. Red iron seals the kiss
      of fire rising with steam.
   The farrier's wrist turning after a hiss
of heat – memories forged from water: winners

wreathed heavy with roses – each fired petal
   bright as the sun. But all that's gone.
      And all that's left is the fresh
        perfume – subtle
   notes of brass riding over retired flesh.
The sun angled on a name etched deep in stone.

'Now of that long pursuit
Comes on at hand the bruit
That Voice is round me like a bursting sea'
— Francis Thompson, *The Hound of Heaven*

'Give to every man that asketh of thee; and of him that taketh away thy
goods ask not again.'
— Luke 6:30

'I have come to realise that the direction I took in April of 1973 was quite
wrong. I persistently, time and again, rejected attractive young women,
who I might have come to love, to make myself the sole servant and slave
of down-and-outs and old people who I did not love. The money and help
that I gave did mostly harm rather than good. I believe 'The Hound of
Heaven' right now is starting to close in on me.'
— George Price, Letter to Kathleen
Price, 5 November, 1974

$$\Delta z = \frac{1}{w}\, cov\,(w_i, z_i) = \frac{1}{3}$$

— Price Equation

settle
        this
rush
    off
the skin's
    pulse

    one hand
        falling

scissors blade
flashing wet

everything else
 given
  to the breath's turbulence
like a tidal wave
swelling and
  folding –
 bore front and whelps
  turning in the collar bone –

 a dark surge of moonlight –
 a dirty celestial charge

rushing between the river banks
  with a crest of names

 washing and rolling out with force
out into estuaries

 and everything

 given back

to the black mouth of the sea

SKIES

1. The Angel
    (Philippe Petit, 7 August 1974)

There is life in a breath of wind.
    And he knows the opposite is true
    and stares down from the clouds –
his body aloft over compact streets of lower Manhattan.
    Greenwich. Liberty. Fulton.
Ángel*! Mensajero de dios!*
    The crowd looking up.
    His silhouette hovering without a shadow.
Concrete. Steel. Glass.
    Shimmering beneath his feet.

2. *Witness*

(Juliane Koepcke, 24 December 1971)

After the fire lost its light and warmth –
the gentle shape peered silently over
      three rows of seats thrown from the wrecked fuselage.
Two miles up in the throat of the night the craft had broken up
and scattered flames into the forest's canopy where the primate had slept waiting
for the dawn.
    Over twisted steel the tamarin watched the girl wake
and moan and draw herself up and drag her feet
    and search and search for something that mattered but could not be found –
the girl searching in a daze then finally dropping her head before leaving.
For days the monkey followed the girl through the forest – over branches –
through vines – the forest claimed by dark boisterous spasms as she huddled by
the bases
    of trees or curled up in cradles of roots till dawn when she followed
snorting crested chickens down to the river where she nursed her wounds
        with screams perfumed with kerosene –
    the sun bright in the sky
   and growing brighter
as though plummeting from another world.

3. Sacrifice
(Laika, 14 April 1958)

Only a few saw the flames mirrored off the ocean.
    A distant ball of dirty light
streaking down from the naked dome of the sky.

And of the few – none were aware of the sacrifice –
    the faint light simply a shooting star –
        a tail of dust burning out above the ship's deck.

o˚,o˚

Eight days into the calm
they watched the sun
rise red off the palm
of the Harmattan.

SPIRIT OF THE FON

'I could not open my mouth because I smelled something terrible.
I heard my daughter snoring in a terrible way, very abnormal.
When crossing to my daughter's bed, I collapsed and fell.'
                                                    – Joseph Nkwain

Lake Nyos, Western High Plateau, Cameroon, 1986

I. Forest Mirror

i.

The moon's eye shifted over the churned water
            and the forest and grasslands rolled wet with nocturnes flowing
    white with myth – a curse from the lake's depth – an ancient breath freed to rise.
Beneath the water the gates had parted – snapping back with fire from a deep
underworld.
            The thunder ball exploding and rising silently. A wave
    snuffing all life in its path – its hypnotic wake too quiet
            and stark to believe – a pale shroud
            from molten lungs. The faulted rock asleep in the arms of the devil's soul.

ii.

Emerald air seals the mountains' shadows.
        Moonlight – cool on simple paths – linking villages to the maar.
    White long-horned cattle low above black volcanic turf: hoof and dung and
    ancient glass.
The forest sings with the sorcery of the earth. The witchery of the sky
            turning shadows into shadows and beasts to humans – then air.
        Where harvest masks rest – millet bowls sit empty –

all without ceremony or wine –
the eye of the moon rolling silently through sleepy plains.

iii.

Here is the altarpiece off water: the moon dissolving to milk.
    The spirit's breath. The spirit – thin and white and pale and almost whole.
Here is the deviant priest rising to fall from the mirror's eye –
a heavy shade – a rushed whisper slipping off a mute's tongue.
    Each dark breath shaped with innocent promises
running through our veins. So we slept.
    Our faith woven into the peace
    of a dream too intimate and sweet to foresee or ever come back from.

II. Subum

In a flat effortless way – the body gives into the freefall.
The eyes calmly close. Each wet collapse robbed of grace.
Pots and crockery ring loud. The steel-clang – communal.
Windows blacken and embers suffocate in the fireplace.

Door to door ugly snores. Guttural gasps. Rubber breaths
above mist-beaded floors where sweating women stood
locked stiff above fufu pots – the air drawing their blood
black – the moon's billowing veil ushering in their death.

Then – the jagged starry absence echoed loud with light.
Each village poisoned by the lake's secret. Tall grass-
fields bowing where scythes once sparkled with the rite
of life – where harvest flutes spindled out notes of glass

that spun in the air then fell like shards of grief into the maar.
The dead were dead. And the hours recoiled as a red sun
rose silently above the compound. The steaming dawn
thinning out – rising dryly beneath the sky's terrible stare.

III.   *Rêves. Musique.*

We loosely rise.
Our shadows unable to wake –
knotted to the uptake like dew –
dawn's music envisioned on air.
The moon sings
and the spirit simmers somewhere –
leaving us with a breath of wings
sprayed with fiery phlegm.
In this dream we are rising through the darkest ascent
where our our minds neither believe in –
nor question –
our breath.

IV. *Returning*

i.

When the rain comes – the flies
disperse with a heavy sickening noise
ringing wild over tangled limbs –
pale wine from blisters and burns
blessed black by hoards suckling
eagerly from the dead's swollen
eyes. Cavernous jaws – once busy
with dark orchestral echoes of
flies now stand brimmed with water.
This rain flushes out odours and
cleanses split flesh. Thick sheets
of loud saturated air shroud each
veiled dawn with rushed dreams
washing fast through lives almost
broken by the *Bad Lake's* curse –
a wall of wet light bridging heaven
and earth with legends of ancestry
and myth. When the rain comes -
it sings off thatch and sings off tin.
Songs sung over body and earth.
The eternal rite of new beginnings.

*

Through dense canopies the rain breaks. The air sluiced with sound.
    Rivers feed miniature tributaries veined over mud-cracked ground.

Streams rumble red – busy with dead insects and leaves flushed out with
the current.

Then silence composes vistas and valleys and rolling hills.
The air flushed with death slipping wet over slippery paths.

ii.

Sun over moon recycles the moon over the sun. Empty huts.
A quietness lingers in the air with the bitter taste of human salts.
The faint smell of abandonment hovers flat where doors crumble beneath lintels
sagging into shadows
where the dead once stood – where
the dead now sing in the constant hold of our hearts.
Sun over moon. Bitter salt of the heart.
Enter now.

iii.

*'First things first: I am neither
shadow nor words – only flesh
could fill these bundled folds of
grief – these torn faded clothes
you once loved – that make me
question what I must look like.
Your daughter says I slip into
the night and sing your name
when I'm asleep – that's bullshit.
She doesn't know me and has
never met you. And all I know
is grief from these hills – these
hills painted red with absences
I could never have expected.
Now every thought fails the old
practices of this deserted place –
this house and these rituals of loss*

sweet in the ache of time falling
sweet off the rote of each breath.
The years have aged me – hoary –
brittle boned. Walking up from
the valley dawn rose and dew bells
dripped off blades of grass – the
grass sharp at my skin – cutting
our shins – my scarred shins
bleeding less than my daughter's.
And I return because I am lost.
Return for the shadowed sunrise.
The shadowed dusk. And walking –
I am afraid and remember your
fingers slipping neatly into mine –
the red broken road burning with
the sun behind us burning with
youthful promise. Who we were
then was the mystery to unfold
and draw us back into a dream
only I would wake from – silence
ringing heavy and loud – heavy
and loud... Soft pulses of sunlight
drip through rotting thatch – ant
mounds pregnant with life stand
pressed into the walls. And I am
here and alone and exhausted by chance –
alone with a daughter who dreams
of you – but will never know who
you are. We stand by the door.
And I set my knee to the ground.
My eyes lost in the empty hearth.'

V.

And if there was an eve of something –
        it was in how the sun set.
           The air liquid and quiet.
    And if there was a quiet fold in the dark –
      it came as the way things were. The way
      children cried.
           The way the moon rose.
             The lake silver without a pulse.

MARTIN

'The dissident does not operate in the realm of genuine power at all. He is not seeking power. He has no desire for office and does not gather votes. He does not attempt to charm the public, he offers nothing and promises nothing.'

Václav Havel

Tuesday

Unaware of his own death Martin woke as though it was any other Tuesday: the blunt electric noise from the bedside clock stirring the darkness that had submerged his body in the warmth of a strange dream that dissipated as soon as he woke.

He sat at the table. Let the kettle whistle longer than usual. Clutched the mug by the handle. And through the rising steam he stared out at the street below where men and women and children appeared in the theatre of his window. He watched them. Walking up and down. Crossing the road. Filtering off into adjoining streets. Heavy coats. Winter on their breaths. Every one of them a nameless character playing a role in this scene governed by the dawn.

He drained his coffee. Dressed and casually descended the stairwell – palming the loose vinyl skin moulded over the iron railings of the banisters. At the exit of the building he stood for a while clutching the worked brass handle of the door and watched the breeze twist into a cold funnel of dirt drilling dryly into the street before spending itself out. Martin tugged the handle of the door. And braced himself for another winter morning in Prague.

The Interview

Only births and funerals come like this –
a cautious glance over newborns or the dead.
And nothing else… The makeup brush was sweeping gently over his face
when a stocky middle aged man burst into the room
slapping the top of his bare wrist with two fingers. Čas!
So the woman finished up and ushered Martin into a room
with a chair from where he caught glimpses of the crew behind the lights.
   And in what seemed no time at all
    he simply formed words
     that to some would not fall away
    as easily as he thought.

Mirror

A closer inspection reveals finer details. The slow dilation of the iris
widening and deepening back into the glass – the iris nothing more
than a portal. And what he sees and feels hold him firm to his stance
as water beneath his toothbrush swirls down the drain with the gurgling
sound of something he had heard in the dream he had woken from.

Ghosts

Sometimes a twin misses the other who came stillborn in a slow muscular flush. So when the crowd dispersed on Národní třída and the body was dragged from the crowd – the seed was sewn. And the next morning Martin sat hunkering over a steaming mug – staring down the streets of Prague where men and women walked briskly as he would soon do along the same street he was staring down – unaware of the fact that he was staring at himself lifting the collars of his winter coat over his nape and crossing the street to begin a journey that would take him to Charles University and further beyond in time.

1. Lost Empires

There is a lighthouse within the Bosphorus Strait
that says everything and nothing – a light
between the Black Sea and the sea of Marmara –
Kiz Kulesi – Leander's Tower – where the wind and the wind's light
draw two continents together.
This thought sits hungry in his head.
The heat singing mischievously with the sun.
Trowel and brush working grit and sand
with a blind mistrust he has come to learn
means nothing more than
the earth simply speaking
back to itself.

2. Ancient Priests

The ritual off the trowel's tongue is spiritual.
The feel of grit beneath his fingertips
leaves him lost somewhere within himself –
the soil rammed with a history of prayers.

3. Cult for the Dead

Beneath these layers –
time's shape rests buried within the hill –
the forensic grind of agricultural toil
preserved in crusted silt.

To the east – memories held by the dead lay flushed with acres of wheat –
vast golden winds that once bowed heavy with grain –
       the valley beneath the plateau
        swathed with stars
scythed by the moon's blade.

John E Mack – 'Something scared you. What Scared you?'
Emma – 'The noise.'
John E Mack – 'What noise?'
Emma – 'The noise we heard in the air.'
John E Mack – 'You heard a noise in the air? What was the noise like?
Was it a roar, a buzz or a hum? What kind of noise?'
Emma – 'It was like someone was blowing the flute.'

Ruwa, Mashonaland East, 1994

She's late and knows she's late and doesn't put her foot down –
but simply cruises as the red disc of the sun hovers in the pale
evening sky – Harare's squat silhouette fading beneath a veil
of dust that clings to the rear windshield like skin. A town-

ship floats by. Then farmland. Then the turnoff where the car's
gearbox screams through each hard shift of the manual change-
down – her grip welded to the steering wheel. It's all too strange
for her. She wonders what Tau would have made of *The Visitors*.

Two years Taurai's been gone. The car stalls in the schoolyard.
The Fiat's dark metallic shell hissing in the grainy light. Everyday
she has left the office late – fearing the drive home. Ever since

The Visitors came – she has had to endure her daughter's hard
edged silences – the cruel spark in the twelve-year-olds eye –
the same glare she gave suffering through her father's absence.

ANTIPODES

The pickup sits parked and cools in the barn.
    Thirteen milk churns silent
after each can sang beneath the stars
    with full aluminium bars
      ringing fat with highland cream –
the road winding down to the stream
where dawn and silt slipped slowly into the valley.

On the shopping street of the small town –
    he met his wife's friend – the butter maker –
      and both exchanged churns
and unloaded and uploaded with each taking turns
      as they'd done for years
      as the sky was rinsed of the dark.
When done – the farmer grabbed the morning paper
    and headed back to the farm –
the stream beneath the bridge pale as a newborn calf's tongue –
    the water lilac and slow
where the pickup crossed through the gates of *Māori Arms* –
    through fields thick with alfalfa
and paddocks checkered with lactating Holstein.
The Hilux entered the barn.
    The smell of coffee from the homestead.
    Waikato Times on the passenger's seat.
      The fresh newsprint lifting and curling
      off swirls of morning air.
        A spark off fire
    in a photograph. A headline
        above the image collapsing
      to enclose the Arab Spring.

'May my enemy be assuaged by these waves
Because they are beautiful even to his evil,
May the drizzle be a benediction to his heart...'

Derek Walcott

'Free diving — plunging to the greatest possible depths on a
single breath without scuba gear — is one of the more extreme
contemporary diversions, and last weekend it cost the 28-year-old
French- woman her life as a world record attempt off the coast of
the Dominican Republic went tragically awry.'

New York Times, 12 October 2002

i.

from the depths
    there is no sound of rain
        meeting the ocean's surface –
only the grand motion of the deep
        hoists his wife in grey columns of sea.
    An arm in the half-light will only take her body halfway.
        Her diving sled abandoned
on the steel line
    where water
flows slower
than the wind's history

ii.

    when the clock
    counts down – the seconds
exceed her time –
    forcing him to dive

iii.

and fill his palms with
        propulsion –
corkscrewing
        and clawing for the ocean's bed.

The weight of water
darkening his blood.
Compressing cavities
and plates of the skull

    iv.

        and

where

    v.

pressure
        condenses air

        he snatches his wife
from another man's arms.
        And cradling her body.
Kicks and kicks.
        And races for the sky.

*'Here, we have a tiny expression of his extraordinary genius distilled down
into something you can hold in your hand.'*
                              -Geoffrey Munn, Antiques Roadshow.

*A flighted full toss on leg stump by a spinner. Any other will play this shot
on leg side by pull shot or glance or flick. But Sachin made a space and
played a perfect cover drive for four.'*
                              – Martin Crowe, cricketer

The signature phrase: the trumpet's brass crescendo
rises bright over a chorus of clarinets. Michael Aspel
stands poised on the parapet of a castle in rural Wales.
A brief introduction displays the grandeur of Powys.
How do they keep the grass so fuckin' green! The ball
turning slowly through the screen – over intact bales –

back to the keeper squatting on his heels. Jackman
comments on the seam after a wry remark by Shastri.
*He began his glassmaking career making perfume
bottles for the Corsican perfumer Coty – I assume
around about… 1910 – but this is earlier. The artistry
is truly breathtaking. How did such a piece come*

into your possession? A fingernail gently nudges
a brooch. A woman battling out of the 20th century
takes her time with words. *You fuckin' god Tendulkar!*
A single run off the second ball of the fiftieth over –
history – a double ton! *And that's real gold? Really?
Yes. The insect's body is formed from pâte de verre.*

The wings from plique-à-jour enamel. The innings
done. *They can't expect to chase this down.* The art –
the clean learned finish – 25 fours – 3 sixes – *faster
than any man! The absolute quality of a true master
at work.* In the background some intellectual fart
in a knitted purple cardigan nods sternly – laughter

emanates somewhere far off in the hall. Everyone
knows the outcome – the local crowd sensing victory –
the glass cicada's polished fire flying over the deck
at Gwalior. *If this went up for auction – this Lalique…
No.* She stops him. Something about family history
falls flash-lit with tickertape over a cardboard cheque.

'Elite (professional) MVD and FSB snipers are trained at the Water Transport Special Police Detachment facilities near Moscow. Famed special units such as the FSB's Alfa detachment and the MVD's Vympel detachment also regularly train here. The school and its graduates get the latest sniper gear to field test, but most stick with the SVD with a silencer. The professional snipers in Chechnya work on the principal of killing the most dangerous enemy first.'

Lester W. Grau & Charles Q. Cutshaw, Infantry, summer 2002

'To serious orchid collectors, danger is value. Most orchid varieties can be easily grown in nurseries, but the plants produced in such conditions suffer from what one dealer describes as 'the stigma of perfection' Their colours may be artificially bright, their petal structure too uniform. Prettified and no challenge to obtain, they lack the sensual, quasi-mystical aura of wild orchids. In the surreal demi-monde of orchidelerium, such plants are imposters.'

William Langley, *The Telegraph*, 2006

1. The Wolf Gates

When the first shot rang out over the northern rift –
  the sky was pale and everything lay stiff and cinereous –
the sun somewhere beneath the horizon – silent in its ascension.
    First the boy fell – clutching his throat –
      the men behind him fanning out –
some fending off the air with their palms – others cupping snow at their hips
and almost swimming – others crouching and searching the sky but never
    finding where the rifleman lay – the skeleton stock
nudging his shoulder with tight coughs.
        One by one they fell.
And before the sun had even caressed the height of the forest.
      The forest was quiet again.

2. Dawn

When Artyom wakes – he finds himself rolled into a ball.
His chin locked deep into his jugular notch. Spine pressed
up against a pelawan trunk. He sifts his fingers through
the warm moist earth and stares out at the world before him.

Rolling over onto his back – he levers his weight off his left
elbow and rests seated with his knees up. His eyesight clears.
The vestibules of his mouth slick and bitter with palm wine.
His heart thudding as though a beast dragged him from his cot –

mauling his soul but wanting very little to do with his flesh.
As he looks up he scans the understory of the forest – a vast
and intricate monochrome sketch of trunks and boughs and
vines and leaves – a grey tangled mass twilight is yet to paint.

In the clearing before him: a nylon shelter cuts a hard dark
edge over indistinct shapes – the taut skirts of a tarpaulin
lashed with guy ropes to abiding trunks. The top of the nylon
sheet apexed to avoid collecting the clear weight of rain.

The camp's fire-pit glows. A nest of feathered ash pulsing
with a weak red pulse. The warm air above the pit warping
dreamily as his mind replays their return to the camp –
      the hike from the black cliffs of the gorge –
Gabriel and Ji-hwan and the guide constantly at each other –
      whispering sharply till Artyom pushed ahead on his own –
         leaving the three men behind – slashing away.

Посмотри на него. Похоже, он ищет призраков.

With the recollection of these words everything blossoms vividly:
      four men by the fire eating without speaking –
the fire's flames reciting ancient hypnotic rhythms of light –

four silhouettes slouched back in the palms of palm wine –
each man transfixed on sparks rising like souls
    fading beneath the dense chlorophyll dome

that rang loud around them with every nocturnal sound –
    the forest's canopy shielding stars from their eyes –
        their eyes drawn heavy by the machete's work.

One after the other they retired to their cots.
    Artyom last – the bass line of the forest thumping through his veins –
his breath easing back – his pulse slowing as dreams rose
    and spiraled up with the arms of sacred vines –

    up into steep mountain trails
    of rock winding high into the sky –
    up into the salt paths of stars

swirling into a single light then falling back
to the valley and parting the forest
with whooping vowels of gibbons' songs –

    the Kapuas sweet with a veil of mist rising
    delicate and clean – its muscled breadth
    flowing through twilight like a glass song.

3. *Vird*

Columns of air. Silent. Thin and faceless.
He watches the nameless rise in one breath –
rising off the river's tongue in a veiled
whisper that whispers up into the open sky.

Darkness has wasted away behind his back
and dawn's brush begins to work on bark
before swabbing colour over foliage. The
forest's nocturne gaining a sharp diurnal pitch.

With time the bald sun gathers its weight
and leans on the black shoulders of the gorge
and stares down the jagged corridor lined
with blind roots clutching naked rocks.

He watches the mist steam off the river.
White then magenta then red. When the sun
leaps high the mist bursts into yellow bars
of heat firing into the blue sky before falling

and becoming the dense green knotted
behind him. He closes his eyes to purge his
mind of the dead. With his eyes closed
he senses the world around him triggered

by light: buds and blossoms anchored by
jewel drops of dew – choruses of creatures
scored on vapours rich with heavy notes –
thick carpets of compost shifting on the forest

floor where armies of insects unpack layers
of dead leaves – this dark incense filtering
out to him – the smells of forest and river
becoming one scent after the mist has gone.

*

With his broad forearm –
he pushed the brambles aside
and stepped off the ledge where yellow flakes of lichen
sprayed out crisp against the white snow.
He climbed down the ledge and made his way to the clearing.
On the border of the clearing he saw the tracks of the she-wolf and looked
east to where the wolf had vanished
and bowed his head and moved on to where the bodies lay –
the clearing swabbed red with the men's last movements.
One man was still alive and dragged himself to a boy who lay still.
He approached the man.
And when the man saw him
and when their eyes met – neither spoke.
He genuflected and placed his left palm
on the man's forehead.
And with his right hand
drew the knife out of its sheath
and pressed the man's head down.

The man's heart quivered
warmly in his palm. He brought the muscle
close to his face. The bright metallic tang entering his nostrils –
the smell igniting a dark thrill in his own heart –
a thrill that forced him to step back.
With blood still wet on his hands he cast the rifle off his shoulder

and walked deep into the forest where he slipped in and out of shadows
for days – where he slept in the frozen darkness –
the air sighing sharp –
cutting at any exposed skin.
Eight weeks he roamed and slept and woke
and read the snow for any trace of human life.
Eight weeks he roamed the forest –
avoiding any trodden path. Walking deeper into the shadows
where he left few tracks and wandered on –
unhinged by the realisation
that he had forgotten his own name.

He wandered through the trees
and walked up the mountain
and found himself on the bare mantel of a ridge.
The ridge twisting off the mountain's shoulder then winding down
to a thicket of elm where snow lay heavy with water trickling
into a gentle song that sang into the valley –
the stream swelling and flowing into the Assa –
the Assa flowing northeast to the wider Sunzha
with the winter sun stark
on its ashen face.
All this thirty years ago
for the man who morphed to every shape –
the man who could run for hours
starved of food and sleep –
the man who knew when his pulse reached its limit –
who took death by the hand and stared death
in the face – daring death to do something different.
This man who stepped off the ledge
and walked to the bodies lying in the snow –
focusing on the wounded man dragging himself
over to his son. This man who locked eyes with the boy's father.

Both men saying nothing.
      Then something blossoming
           when the sound of steel slipped off
    the hide of the stiff sheaf –
the knife's blade then working
      hard and fast –
unlike the delicate work when blind roots
      are lifted from moss
    and stone.

4. *Paphiopedilum Kolopukingii*
   Journal entry, 12 October 2016

i.

The vernacular of the Kalimantan has not been easy.

The forest thick after the New Year Monsoon.

The sky heavy and loud and warm – becoming cold

as evening-showers wash everything over till dawn.

And successive dawns come with the same deluge –

the constant downpour linking the heavens and earth –

tears of gods softening the forest floor with secret

rivers flowing beneath the humus carpet underfoot.

When the deluge stops – a wild silence reigns over

vast stretches of trees cushioned by rich undergrowth.

And for a while everything for miles holds still

and stark – so still the entire forest could be dead.

A stillness arresting the breath – till the breath sucks

back deep and hard like the first breath ever drawn.

ii.

I can't forget what the old man said in the village –

his words continuously reverberating in my head

Ketika orang meninggal di jantung hutan,
langit selalu absen dari pandangan mereka.

spirits roaming through mazes unknown to all but

plants and creatures of the evolving underworld –

the dead being part of the understory's breath before

departing in private ascensions over towering

emergent shapes – shapes woven into the fabric

of something vast beyond the scope of the sky.

Perhaps it's these lost souls who seed the forests

with frail blooms drawing strength from atavistic

barks and sacred cliffs – blessing them with breaths

as they search thickets and vines for clearings –

the wind brushing off leafs and sifting through

shadows with the distant perfume of diesel oil.

iii.

Then the old man spoke of an ancient god falling

from the sky – and the god's velvet feathers scattering

over hardened shapes – the god spending time

on earth with men who knew nothing of pure beauty.

And in her rage – the god finally rose – and rose

with petals of fire falling in the wake of her flight

leaving the earth and mortals to remember her forever.

Gabriel and Ji-hwan take all this with a grain of salt –

Lomonosov graduates. Journalists out here to get

something good on the *mad veteran* in Borneo

still haunted by screaming villages burning beneath

dirty clouds of smoke – valleys torn and littered with limbs –

the heights of Caucasian mountains shivering with trees…

And the two men will lift their glasses in a bar overlooking

The Moskva – their piece tagged with names of warlords

who sent hail over broken hills to churn fields as villagers

fled in droves for Ingushetia. And though the Moscovite

and Koroyo saram know I dream of those who ran from

incendiary rain – running into the scope of our aim –

they don't know that I too wish to be buried beneath

a stone without a name – where a single flower burgeons

from blind roots that felt through stony soil to find a cup

of bone – the cavity of my skull compact with secrets.

My ribs will be collapsed. My bones leached of minerals.

And my soul lost somewhere above a field where lone

wolf calls echo between Chiri-Yurt and Duba-Yurt.

5. The Wolf

He lay still.
The muzzle trained on the clearing where birch shadows
fanned out north above a blank pan of snow.
   Two days he lay rigid – cushioned by stone –
    studying the brisk winter light on the ledge below.

 The air was crisp. Sterile.
No fowl. Fox. Roe deer. Nothing. Only the outline of a goshawk
once from above – its shadow disappearing into a silver-barred route
   where the moon's sickle sheared three dawns –
the smoke from burnt oils and burnt timber riding stiff off the air –
 the earth of village cemeteries too hard to break.

As dawn broke – a young she-wolf slid into the clearing –
   casting a shadow only a ghost could throw.
 Each swift movement silently woven
with the energy of a spirit passing through the ether of a forgotten world.
  Sharp eyes peering everywhere. Virgin pelt slipping through trees
with a silver flow – the air white on her breath.
After the wolf slipped off and vanished – he didn't wait long
 before the boy appeared. He lifted the rifle
  and captured the young face in the lens.
   The boy fell. The men behind him fanned out.
   Then fell and coloured the snow.

Acknowledgments are due to the editors of the following journals who first published versions of these poems: *Cyphers*, *Poetry International*, *Poetry London*, *The International Journal of Law and Society* and *The White Review*.

The author would like to express his gratitude to Lancaster Park, the New York Public Library, the Dorothy and Lewis B. Cullman Center for Scholars and Writers, the Prince Bernhard Fund & Ludo Pieters Gastschrijver Fonds, the Rockefeller Foundation and Rolex Arts Initiative.

Particular thanks to Jane Morris, Brian Jones, Magda Pavitt, Ellah Wakatama, Murray McCartney, Irene Staunton, Michael Schmidt, Tracy K. Smith, Michael Ondaatje, Simon Armitage, Andrew Latimer, Rumbi Katedza and Patience & Zenzo Lusengo.